But what is marketing anyway?

Layout, revision, and cover design: Expressa Livros.
www.expressalivros.com.br

Translation of the book "Mas o que é marketing afinal?", originally written in Brazilian Portuguese.

Richard Souza

But what is marketing anyway?

expressa
livros

All rights reserved.

Partial or total reproduction of the content of this work is prohibited without the prior express authorization of the author.

Notice: The author of this manual sought to ensure the accuracy of the information, but different definitions may exist, as well as variations in the effectiveness of methods and strategies. The possibility of human error in preparing this material is also not ruled out.

Dedication:

I dedicate this book to everyone who seeks to understand more about marketing.

Summary

Preface

Marketing is a fascinating subject, with multiple applications and constant evolution. It encompasses various concepts and there are different understandings, often leading to confusion about what is or isn't "marketing."

We can say that marketing is continuously adapting to changes in consumer behavior and market trends, incorporating new strategies that emerge with new technologies. It is crucial knowledge for personal and business success.

In this book, different definitions of marketing are presented, ranging from the most traditional to the most recent, from the academic to the popular, with the aim of providing a comprehensive view and helping to answer the question that gives the book its title: "But what is marketing, after all?"

Each definition presented in this book offers a perspective on what marketing is and how it can be applied in different contexts, presenting different types of "marketing."

In this book, we will be "discussing" marketing, covering everything from the most traditional and didactic definitions to the vision and examples of marketing applications in various areas, such as personal marketing, political marketing, election marketing, affiliate marketing, content marketing, digital marketing, trade marketing, etc.

I hope this book helps readers understand what marketing is, its different applications and variations, the different approaches to marketing, and choose the most suitable strategies for their objectives.

In order to cater to all audiences, this book will always strive to avoid extremely technical terms unfamiliar to the non-specialized public, often adopting its own terminology to make the understanding of the ideas more universally accessible.

May this book help you understand what marketing is and inspire you to forge new paths for the success of your personal or professional projects.

Have a good read!

The author.

Definitions of Marketing

There are many definitions of marketing, from different authors and perspectives. Below, we will see some of the most well-known ones.

According to the definition approved by the American Marketing Association (AMA) in 2017, "marketing is the activity, set of institutions, and processes for creating, communicating, delivering, and exchanging offerings that have value for consumers, clients, partners, and society at large."

On the other hand, one of the most renowned authors in this field, Philip Kotler, states that "Marketing is a social process by which individuals and groups obtain what they need and desire through creating, offering, and exchanging products and services of value with others."

But those are not the only definitions of marketing. We have other definitions from other significant authors as well.

In the first edition of his book "Basic Marketing: A Managerial Approach" published in 1960, Jerome McCarthy defined marketing as "the performance of business activities that direct the flow of goods and services from producer to consumer or user."

Peter Drucker, known as the father of modern management, understood marketing as "the business function that identifies unsatisfied needs and wants, measures their magnitude and potential profit, specifies which target markets will be best served by the company, and decides on appropriate products, services, and programs to serve these markets."

Theodore Levitt, a former professor at Harvard Business School and the author of the term "marketing myopia," which criticizes companies that focus more on their products and services than on the desires and needs of consumers, understood marketing as "the creation and delivery of a set of benefits that exceed customers' expectations and create lasting relationships with them."

As for ChatGPT (OpenAI, 2023), an artificial intelligence, it defines marketing as "a set of strategies and actions that seek to understand, influence, and satisfy the needs and desires of a specific target audience through the offering of products, services, or ideas that add value and are relevant to that audience."

In some Brazilian university courses, marketing is sometimes translated to Portuguese as "mercadologia," although "mercadologia" can be understood as a more limited field focused on market analysis and research (which is part of marketing). However, marketing and mercadologia are often accepted as synonyms or simple translations.

These different definitions do not contradict each other. They complement and/or confirm each other, but they are just a part of the possible answers to what marketing truly is.

In popular culture, there are many other understandings of what this English word, "marketing," means without translation. Some even use the word "marketing" negatively, as if it were synonymous with "false advertising," using the expression "that's just marketing" to refer to something that falsely claims advantages, for example.

Of course, marketing is not synonymous with false advertising, it's worth emphasizing...

For others, marketing would be synonymous with selling online. However, marketing is not only about selling, nor is it limited to the online world. Marketing practices were already adopted in the medieval era, although it only began to emerge as a formal discipline during the Industrial Revolution.

Although marketing may seem like a new topic to many, one of the most well-known articles on the subject, published under the title "The Management of Marketing Costs" by James Culliton, dates back to 1948...

But we have yet to provide a clear, objective, and complete answer to the question that gives the book its title. So, to ease the natural anticipation for the answer, we will say, for now, that Marketing is all of that and much more.

"Traditional Marketing" vs "Digital Marketing"

When the internet started being used for marketing purposes, there was a need, at that moment, to differentiate the marketing practices that existed until then from the marketing that began to utilize the internet. Thus, this differentiation emerged, and the terms "Traditional Marketing" and "Digital Marketing" began to be used, separating internet-based marketing from offline marketing.

Some people may initially think that this separation considers the difference between the physical or tangible medium and the non-physical or intangible medium. However, upon further reflection, it becomes easy to realize that so-called "digital marketing" is no less physical than marketing in a television commercial or through telephone calls (telemarketing). And these means (television and telephone) are still attributed to "traditional marketing."

So, being physical or not is not the differentiating factor that distinguishes what is called "Traditional Marketing" from what is called "Digital Marketing."

Following our reasoning, we can find the obvious explanation that the differentiating factor lies in being "digital," that is, being on the internet and utilizing digital tools and technologies.

Okay... This explanation may be correct. But it still doesn't justify the separation between marketing conducted through any other medium and marketing conducted "on the internet, utilizing digital tools and technologies."

Marketing done using television is not separated from the "traditional," marketing done using paper pamphlets is not separated from the "traditional," marketing done through telephone calls is not separated from the "traditional,"...

So, what prompted this separation was the novelty of using the internet and digital tools and technologies? Also...

"Digital Marketing" emerged with significant impact and its unique characteristics. Without a doubt, "Digital Marketing" does exist, and it has great potential.

But then, why question the separation between "Traditional Marketing" and "Digital Marketing"?

Currently, "Digital Marketing" is no longer a novelty; it is an important medium for practically any marketing plan.

But what is the so-called "Traditional Marketing" today, considering that it is difficult to imagine a marketing plan that doesn't include the internet, digital tools, and technologies?

Well... The question I invite you to reflect upon is the relevance today of understanding digital marketing as an alternative to non-digital marketing, as if the integration of digital and non-digital strategies is not the current "traditional" or the current standard.

In conclusion, dividing marketing into traditional and digital may not be the most accurate division in present times. Perhaps it makes more sense today to replace the idea of the existence of "Traditional Marketing" without digital elements with a broader concept of Marketing, which includes both digital and non-digital aspects in their different types and strategies, frequently blending the digital and non-digital, physical and virtual...

Therefore, in this book, whenever the word "marketing" is mentioned without qualifiers, the text will refer to marketing in a broad sense, including what some call traditional and what some call digital because marketing encompasses all of that and much more.

Marketing Strategies

Just as there are many definitions of marketing, there are also various marketing strategies. These marketing strategies can also be known as "marketing approaches," "marketing modalities," "marketing tactics," "types of marketing," and "specific types of marketing," among other expressions. However, the term "marketing strategies" has been chosen as it is believed to better define what will be addressed.

Below are some examples of marketing strategies, along with a brief definition of each of these strategies.

Affiliate Marketing:

A strategy that involves the use of partners and affiliates to promote products and services through a rewards program based on commissions for generated sales.

Attraction Marketing:

Also known as inbound marketing, it is a strategy that aims to attract customers through relevant and personalized content, rather than interruptions or intrusive advertisements.

Search Marketing:

A strategy that involves optimizing content for search engines like Google, with the goal of improving brand visibility on search engine results pages.

Cause Marketing:

Focused on social, environmental, or political causes, seeking to generate value for society and improve the brand's image through supporting a cause.

Content Marketing:

Creates and distributes relevant and valuable content to attract and engage a specific target audience.

Visual Content Marketing:

Involves creating and sharing visual content such as images, videos, and infographics to engage and entertain the audience, increase brand visibility, and strengthen the relationship with consumers.

CRM Marketing:

Involves the use of customer relationship management technologies to monitor, segment, and personalize company interactions with its customers, aiming to improve customer satisfaction, loyalty, and profitability.

Data Marketing or Data-Driven Marketing:

Involves the collection, analysis, and use of consumer data to personalize offers and the shopping experience, aiming to improve the effectiveness of marketing campaigns. It is used in personalized marketing, for example.

Differentiation Marketing:

It is the strategy in which a company seeks to differentiate its product or service from competitors, aiming to create a perception of superior value compared to competitors. This differentiation can be achieved through product or service quality, differentiated customer service, etc.

E-commerce Marketing:

It is marketing for selling products or services online, in e-commerce. Digital marketing techniques are used in this strategy.

Ambush Marketing:

A strategy that involves promoting a brand or product at events sponsored by competitors, seeking to steal the audience's attention and generate buzz around the brand.

Energy Marketing:

It is the strategy in which a company seeks to create enthusiasm around its product or service, generating greater visibility and involvement from the audience with the product or service. It is usually adopted in product launches and exploits the consumer's emotional engagement.

Event Marketing:

Promotes products and services through live events such as conferences, fairs, and exhibitions.

Exclusivity Marketing:

A strategy that involves offering exclusive, limited, or differentiated products or services, with the aim of creating perceived value for the customer and generating interest and desire to purchase.

Experience Marketing:

Focused on creating unique and memorable experiences for customers, with the aim of increasing loyalty and the brand's reputation.

Export Marketing:

A strategy focused on exporting products and services to other countries, including adapting the offer to the needs and preferences of foreign consumers.

Loyalty Marketing:

Seeks to maintain and strengthen the relationship with current customers by offering exclusive and personalized benefits, such as loyalty programs, discounts, and special promotions.

Demand Generation Marketing:

It is marketing aimed at generating or increasing demand for a product or service. It includes actions that seek to present the product or service to the consumer by highlighting its features, qualities, and usefulness, making it desired by the consumer.

Guerrilla Marketing:

Involves creative and impactful actions, usually low-cost, aimed at capturing the audience's attention and generating buzz around the brand.

Influence Marketing:

Uses digital influencers to promote products and services through their social media and other channels.

Niche Influence Marketing:

As the name suggests, it is a strategy that uses an influencer from a specific niche to which the product or service is targeted.

Social Influence Marketing:

Involves collaborating with influential people on social networks to promote products or services, leveraging their credibility and reach to reach a wider audience and increase brand visibility.

Influencer Marketing:

A strategy that involves the use of digital influencers to promote products and services, aiming to reach the target audience and increase brand.

But What Is Marketing Anyway?

In the previous chapters, you encountered classical definitions of marketing, as well as reflections on related concepts. You also came across various examples of marketing strategies, all of which, in a way, contribute to a possible answer to what marketing is.

Marketing encompasses everything you have seen in the previous chapters and much more...

It is a powerful tool for promoting causes, individuals, businesses, ideas, and more. It is also a science to be studied, constantly evolving according to some authors, or an art that relies on creativity and intuition according to others.

And yes, marketing is all that and much more.

Like any tool, it can be used positively or negatively, efficiently or inefficiently, leading to success or failure. It always depends on the motivation of the user, their mastery of techniques, and the strategic choices they make to achieve their objectives.

This book does not aim to provide a new and definitive answer to the question in its title. It was written to offer readers an initial perspective on marketing as a foundation for their own construction of the answer to the question: "But What Is Marketing Anyway?"

Marketing Glossary

Advertising Campaign: A series of advertisements or advertising pieces created to promote a product or service over a specific period of time.

Avatar: A fictional representation of the ideal customer used to guide marketing strategy.

Benchmarking: The process of comparing a company's results with those of other leading companies in the same industry to improve performance.

Brand Equity: The value that a brand represents to consumers beyond its products or services.

Branding: The process of building and managing a brand, including its name, logo, visual identity, and market positioning.

Call-to-Action (CTA): A call to action, inviting the user to perform a specific action, typically aimed at converting a potential customer into an actual customer. It can be a phrase or button that encourages the audience to take a specific action, such as subscribing to a newsletter or purchasing a product.

Customer Acquisition Cost (CAC): The total amount a company spends to acquire a new customer.

Churn Rate: The rate at which customers cancel a product or service.

Conversion: Each successful outcome of a marketing campaign, usually the number of website visitors who take a desired action, such as filling out a form or making a purchase. Used to generate the "conversion rate."

Cost Per Acquisition (CPA): The average cost to acquire a new customer.

Cost-Per-Click (CPC): The average cost paid for each click on an advertisement.

Cost Per Mille (CPM): The average cost per thousand impressions of an advertisement. The term "cost-per-thousand" can also be used in English with the same meaning.

Customer Relationship Management (CRM): A system or strategy that manages a company's interactions with its customers.

Digital Influencer: A person who has a large following on social media and can influence the purchasing decisions of their followers.

Engagement: Interaction between a company and its customers, including likes, comments, shares, and messages.

Inbound Marketing: A marketing approach that focuses on attracting customers through useful and relevant content, rather than interruptive advertising.

Keyword: A word or phrase that summarizes the content of a web page and is used for search engine optimization (SEO).

Key Performance Indicator (KPI): Metrics used to evaluate the performance of a marketing campaign, such as conversions, traffic, or reach. It is usually referred to in the plural (KPIs) since multiple indicators are used.

Lead: A potential customer who has shown interest in a product or service. It is completely different from the meaning of "lead" in journalism.

Lead Generation: The process of attracting and capturing contact information from potential customers.

Marketing Automation: The use of tools and technologies to automate marketing processes, such as email campaigns and campaign management.

Marketing Mix: Also known as the 4 Ps, it consists of product, price, promotion, and place, which are the main variables that a company can control to influence the demand for its products or services.

Persona: Fictional characters created to represent different types of buyers who may be interested in a company's products or services, including demographic, behavioral, and psychological

Reach: The number of people who have seen a marketing campaign or content.

Sales Funnel: A model that represents the stages a potential customer goes through before becoming an actual customer, typically divided into three phases: top of the funnel (awareness), middle of the funnel (consideration), and bottom of the funnel (decision).

SWOT Analysis: An acronym for "strengths," "weaknesses," "opportunities," and "threats." It is a market analysis tool used to evaluate the strengths and weaknesses of a company, as well as the opportunities and threats in the external environment.

References

OpenAI. **ChatGPT, natural language model.** Available at: https://openai.com/blog/chat-gpt-3/. Accessed on January 30, 2023.

AMERICAN MARKETING ASSOCIATION (AMA). **The Definition of Marketing: What is Marketing?**. Disponível em: https://www.ama.org/the-definition-of-marketing-what-is-marketing/. Acesso em: 30 jan. 2023.

KOTLER, Philip; KELLER, Kevin Lane. **Administração de marketing**. 15. ed. São Paulo: Pearson, 2015.

DRUCKER, Peter F. **Administração: tarefas, responsabilidades, prática**. São Paulo: Pioneira, 2002.

LEVITT, Theodore. **A imaginação de marketing**. São Paulo: Atlas, 1985.

MCCARTHY, Jerome E. **Basic Marketing: A Managerial Approach**. Homewood, Illinois: Irwin, 1964.

www.ingramcontent.com/pod-product-compliance
Lightning Source LLC
Chambersburg PA
CBHW060022300526
45794CB00003B/1262